NOLS

River Rescue

NOLS
River Rescue

Essential Skills
for Boaters

Nate Ostis
Illustrations by Frank Preston

STACKPOLE
BOOKS

Published by
STACKPOLE BOOKS
5067 Ritter Road
Mechanicsburg, PA 17055
www.stackpolebooks.com

Printed in the United States of America

First edition

10 9 8 7 6 5 4 3 2 1

Cover design by Caroline Stover
Cover photograph courtesy of Brad Christensen/NOLS

Library of Congress Cataloging-in-Publication Data

Ostis, Nate.
  NOLS river rescue : essential skills for boaters / Nate Ostis ;
illustrations by NOLS instructor, Frank Preston. — 1st ed.
      p. cm.
  Includes index.
  ISBN-13: 978-0-8117-3352-6 (alk. paper)
  ISBN-10: 0-8117-3352-1 (alk. paper)
  1. Boats and boating—Safety measures. 2. Rescue work. I.
National Outdoor Leadership School (U.S.) II. Title.
  GV777.55.O77 2010
  797.10289—dc22

                                                      2009031229

Contents

Introduction

NOLS has been running river courses across the world since 1965. The ideas, concepts, and systems illustrated in this book are a sampling of the risk management and rescue skills we believe are fundamental to traveling on moving water. If a technique isn't in this book, that doesn't mean it doesn't work. This book is not an adequate substitute for formal instruction in river rescue; this book is intended to *supplement* formal instruction. Readers are strongly encouraged to take both a practical hands-on river rescue course and a wilderness first-aid course prior to recreating anywhere in or around rivers. These courses typically range from one to three days and instill a great deal of confidence and understanding in the students who take them. Perhaps the greatest benefit of rescue education is the emphasis on preventing emergencies from ever happening in the first place. This is a key component in a fun and enjoyable river wilderness experience.

River Anatomy
AND HYDROLOGY

RATING AND ASSESSING RIVERS
When traveling in, on, and around rivers, you need a firm understanding of hydrology and a river's anatomy. With a few exceptions, most rivers and rapids are rated using the following classification system.

Please note that although the American Canoe Association provides a description for each classification level, whitewater paddlers should develop their own judgment and interpretation of the difficulty of any given rapid. One person's Class II is another person's Class III. Confining the classification system into any proposed collection of descriptions is a limiting approach to the endless varieties and forms of gradient discovered on river systems. Enjoy discussions with others but challenge yourself to decide for yourself what class a given rapid may be. Use some of the following elements as factors in coming to a determination.

TRADITIONAL CLASS I–VI SCALE
for River Ratings and Rapid Classifications

(from the American Canoe Association: www.americancanoe.org)

Class I: Basic. Moving water with a few riffles and small waves.

Class II: Novice. Straightforward rapids with wide, clear channels that are obvious without scouting. Some maneuvering required.

Class III: Intermediate. Rapids with high, irregular waves that are difficult to avoid and capable of swamping an open canoe. Eddies and currents are more powerful. Scouting is often advisable for inexperienced groups.

Class IV: Advanced. Long, difficult rapids with constricted passages that often require precise maneuvering in turbulent waters. Scouting from shore is often necessary, and conditions make rescue difficult.

Class V: Expert. Extremely difficult, long, violent rapids with highly congested routes that nearly always must be scouted from shore. Rescue conditions are difficult, and there is significant hazard to life in the event of a mishap.

Class VI: Extreme & Exploratory. Difficulties of Class V carried to the extreme of navigability. Nearly impossible and very dangerous. For teams of experts, only after close study has been made and all precautions have been taken.

Gradient

How steep is the river? Gradient increases the velocity of water but decreases its depth. It is typically measured in feet per mile in the United States, but many other countries measure it in meters per kilometer. Determining the gradient scale associated with a river description is a key component in evaluating the class number. Generally speaking, the steeper the river, the more challenging the terrain. Be mindful, however, of gradients given for a river's description, as they are often the average of all miles. For example, a river may have an average gradient of 10 feet per mile for a 10-mile section of river. But that could be 9 miles of very flat river with a 90-foot waterfall along the way disguised as an average gradient of 10 feet per mile. Gradient gives a general picture of a river's character.

Volume

How much water is in the river? Typically measured in cubic feet per second (CFS) or cubic meters per second (CMS), the volume of water in a river increases its velocity and depth and has a dramatic effect on the character of the river. One cubic foot is about one milk crate of volume, so 1,000 CFS means about 1,000 milk crates of water are passing a given point every second. One cubic meter equals approximately 35 cubic feet. Some drainages measure volume off established riverside gauges, and the USGS website offers real-time data on most drainages that have those gauges. You'll need to translate such gauge readings into approximate CFS or CMS, so a little research into the area you'll be traveling is highly recommended for an accurate prediction of the volume of water you may encounter at any given time of year.

Constrictions

Is there a narrowing in the riverbed? Constrictions increase velocity much like a thumb over the end of a garden hose. Many rapids are formed by constrictions, often from accumulated debris and deposits at the confluence of a feeding tributary.

River Hazards

What do we need to be aware of? Being able to distinguish river hazards is an essential skill set to develop when running rivers. Seemingly meaningless features in otherwise flat current can be deadly. Strainers, undercuts, sieves, debris, rebar, foot entrapment, remoteness, and water temperature are some of the basic hazards that travelers should learn to identify.

UNDERSTANDING RIVER HAZARDS

This section defines typical river hazards and explains some techniques you need to master to effectively mitigate these hazards.

Strainers

Strainers are objects in a river that do not impede the flow of water but can catch solid objects such as floating logs or people. The most common strainers are trees, shrubs, and tree roots. Although they can be found anywhere on a river, they are usually found on the outside of bends. Trees and shrubs along the riverbank sometimes grow in the water or hang over the water, creating hazards. Likewise, large fallen trees floating in the river at high water can act as strainers.

The best tactic with strainers is to avoid them if at all possible. If a strainer is identified downstream, try to stay clear of it by paddling or swimming away aggressively. If you find yourself heading quickly toward a strainer

When strainers are unavoidable, turn toward them and swim aggressively.

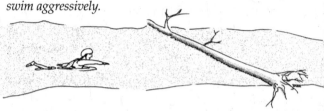

Kick hard to get your body on the surface of the water. It is especially important to get your legs as high as possible.

Pull your body up and over the log before the current pulls your legs under it.

while swimming, turn over on your stomach, and with your head downstream, swim aggressively toward the strainer and climb on top of it (see illustration). Act as if you are trying to do a pushup and get your hips on top of the strainer. This can help prevent your feet from being pulled underneath the strainer while keeping your head above water. This is a risky move that may be your last resort. Many organized river rescue classes practice this move in a controlled setting.

Undercut Rocks, Ledges, and Sieves
Undercut rocks or ledges occur when water wears away at the rock or a bank, leaving a larger portion above the waterline and a smaller, narrower portion below the waterline. These are dangerous because a swimmer or a boat can be pushed under them and get stuck.

The number of undercuts you might encounter depends on the geological makeup of an area. Sedimentary rock tends to erode more quickly, so rivers that flow through it have more undercuts. Undercut rocks and banks are usually found on the outside of bends.

You can sometimes spot an undercut on the upstream side of a rock by the absence of a pillow, or water that usually builds up against the rock, climbing high onto the rock before falling back onto itself. Pillows are sometimes foamy with aerated water. With undercut rocks, the oncoming water has little to no resistance, slipping underneath the overhanging rock.

Undercuts, like strainers, should be avoided. A sieve—a pile of rocks or debris with water flowing through it—allows water to pass through but traps solid objects. Paddle or swim aggressively away from undercuts and sieves. This is a great reason to develop your swimming technique and strength, so you can self-rescue.

Foot Entrapment
Downstream currents can easily push over a standing person whose foot is trapped on the river bottom, typically between boulders or sunken logs. This can happen in relatively mild currents. To reduce the chances of foot entrapment, do not stand in moving water to arrest your downstream progress until the water depth is well below your knees. Keep your feet up when swimming in shallow, rocky rivers.

The defensive swim position, with toes up, is effective in avoiding foot entrapment.

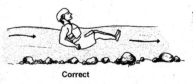

Correct

Incorrect

Rocks above and below the Surface

To see rocks just under the surface, look for some type of disturbance on the surface of the water. When paddling, look downstream and pick a path on the river that avoids rocks and surface disturbances. If hitting or coming up against a rock is unavoidable, aggressively lean the boat into the rock. This exposes the hull of the boat, instead of the deck, to the oncoming current, decreasing the chances of it wrapping around or pinning against the rock. Continue to lean the boat into the rock while you use your upper body strength to work your way around the rock.

RIVER FEATURES AND ANATOMY
Current

Laminar flow refers to smoothly flowing layers of water rather than turbulent ones. Micro-currents swirl between layers, but in general, rivers have distinct jets of water moving downstream, layer upon layer. The fastest water channel in a river is in the center at the top, and the slowest layer is on the edges due to friction along the sides.

Helical flow generally occurs along the riverbanks where fast water meets slow water.

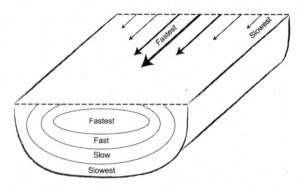

Laminar flow means smoothly flowing layers of water. Note that the outermost layer of water is slowed by friction from the riverbed surface, and the surface layer is susceptible to slower speeds and redirection due to friction with air, wind, and waves.

The result is squirrelly whirlpool water filled with turbulence and vortices rather than laminar flow. Often water in the helical flow will dive deeper into the current in eddy lines while resurfacing downstream in large boils. Helical flow can present a swimmer with difficult challenges when attempting to swim back to shore. The whirlpool-like nature tends to push swimmers and boats back toward the main current.

Centrifugal force causes deeper, faster currents on the outside of a bend and shoals

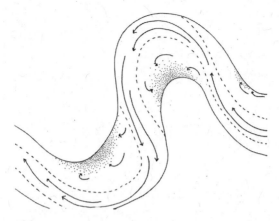

Centrifugal force causes deeper, faster currents on the outside of a bend in the river and shoals, or shallows, on the inside of a bend.

(shallows) on the inside of a bend. Strainers typically establish themselves on the outside of a bend where there are deeper, faster currents. The river carves out the foundation of earth and rock beneath the trees until they finally collapse into the current, forming strainers.

A major constriction in the river channel increases water velocity. When fast water meets slow water, laminar flow is disrupted, resulting in whirlpools, turbulence, and vortices.

Eddies

Eddies, relatively calm pockets of water, form on the downstream side of solid objects, such as rocks or part of the riverbank that juts out into the current. The obstruction creates a barrier in the current, deflecting water around it, and gravity fills the eddy with water. The difference between the main current and the slower eddy current is called the eddy line. The speed in which the eddy water travels back upstream can vary considerably. When there is a notable gradient difference between the eddy water and the main current, the eddy line is sometimes referred to as an eddy fence due to its wall-like appearance. Calmer eddies can make wading across a river easier or stop downstream progress when paddling. As we become better boaters, we become more adept at catching eddies to park our boat for a while.

Waves

Generally speaking, waves are created when water flows over some type of obstruction. Waves vary in size, shape, and behavior. They can be smooth or breaking, flat or steep, stationary or dynamic, predictable or ever-changing. All waves have a trough, face, and

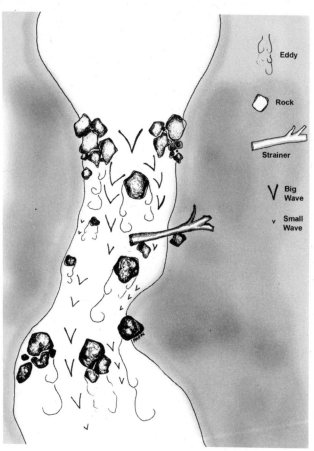

Eddy

Rock

Strainer

V Big Wave

v Small Wave

This map of a section of river shows the difference between eddies and the main current. Eddies are good spots to slow or stop downstream progress for a rest or in case of an emergency.

peak, or crest. Often an obstruction in the riverbed will create the first big wave and a train of subsequent waves will follow behind. This is often referred to as a wave train.

Holes and Hydraulics

Holes (also referred to somewhat synonymously as hydraulics, reversals, stoppers, pour-overs, keepers, and low-head dams) are created when water goes over a submerged object, such as a rock or ledge. (This is different than an eddy, which is created when water flows *around* a rock. A rock can create an eddy at lower water levels and a hole at higher water levels.) Water hits the river bottom on

Sticky Hole (side view)

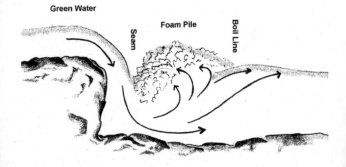

the downstream side and flows back on itself, opposite the direction of the main current. Depending on how large the hole is, the resulting current can be quite strong and may be able to hold buoyant objects, such as a boat or swimmer. Beginner paddlers should try to avoid large holes, but if you cannot, try to paddle through them quickly head on to expose less surface area of your boat to the current of the hole.

Having a clear understanding of river anatomy and hydrology is the foundation of successful river crossings and rescues. The next step for safe river travel is to refine your leadership and judgment skills.

Risk
MANAGEMENT

No matter how skilled you or your group is, you should always have a risk management briefing before going out on the river. All trip members need to understand the hazards of negotiating rivers. Managing these hazards takes active participation from everyone. The briefing should inform the group of potential hazards they might encounter and actions they can take to help manage or avoid those hazards.

Likewise, practice and demonstrate basic safety skills before going out on the water. Review this information as needed so that group members have a thorough understanding of subjective and objective hazards and methods to manage risks. All group members need to be aware of the big picture and be able to manage risk and practice sound decision-making. If one member of the group takes unnecessary risks or shows disrespect for the power of rivers, other members might follow suit. Establish concrete guidelines as a group prior to embarking on the trip and adhere to them throughout the expedition.

EQUIPMENT CONSIDERATIONS

PFDs

While boating, all participants should wear personal flotation devices (PFDs). Size and fit PFDs for each individual before leaving for the field, and wear them properly—secure all zippers, buckles, and ties correctly. The shoulders of the PFD should not come up above the wearer's ears when pulled upward. Take care of PFDs so they work properly: Avoid sitting or standing on them as this compresses the closed-cell foam and abrades the fabric. Store all PFDs in a clean, dry place.

Helmets

Whenever you use a PFD, you should also consider wearing a well-fitted whitewater helmet, especially in a rescue scenario or when paddling anything harder than Class I rapids. The helmet should be securely fastened for a snug, comfortable fit. You should not be able to rock the helmet backward, exposing the

SAFETY TALK OUTLINE

PFD & Helmets
- When to wear them and when you can take them off
- Proper fastening, fit, and care

Footwear
- Appropriate river wear vs. appropriate off-river wear

Basic River Hazards
- Strainers, undercuts, large holes, wave trains, sieves, and rocks
- Foot entrapment
- Getting pinned (Any sensation of pinning means get out of the boat fast.)
- Rapids and "challenge by choice" (You don't have to run any rapid you don't want to.)

Swimming
- Self Rescue: Defensive vs. aggressive techniques and when each is appropriate
- How to maintain spatial awareness and to hear rescuers' commands
- Proximity to your craft

Throw Bags

- Design, use, and care
- How to hold on to the rope and when to let go
- Rope entrapment concerns

River Signals

- Stop, All Clear, Left, Right, Emergency, Are you OK?, Eddy Out
- Paddle, hand, and whistle blasts as signals
- Importance of passing signals on to rest of group

Group Travel

- Trip awareness, including other groups, jet boats, and complacency
- Boat spacing between lead and sweep boats
- Location of rescue gear, first-aid supplies, SAT phones, and radios
- Safety in camp and when walking along shore (Most river accidents occur on shore.)

forehead to potential harm. Chinstraps with Y-formation attachment points are designed to prevent this from happening: One anchor point is slightly behind the ear and the other slightly in front of the ear.

Footwear

Make sure your footwear will stay on your feet at all times while in, on, and around the river. Statistics show that a majority of river accidents occur when traveling on foot along the slippery, unstable shoreline. Good footwear also helps protect your feet if you slip accidentally while wading or unexpectedly fall from your boat. Wearing footwear in the boat, too, speeds up response time should you have to get out of your boat and help another boater.

Throw Bags

A throw bag is a small bag with a rope stuffed in it, often used to toss to an accidental swimmer and pull him back to the boat. Throw bags are an essential piece of boating gear. They come in lengths of 10 to 25 meters (30 to 80 feet) and widths of ¼ to ⅜ inches. Strengths vary from 500 to 2,500 kg (1,000 to 5,000 pounds). Kayakers use little throw bags that are convenient on a small craft. Many professional raft guides use throw bags with longer, heavier ropes that can also be used in haul systems. Ropes can be made of nylon, polyester, polypropylene, or Kevlar.

RIVER SIGNALS

It can sometimes be very difficult to hear on the river, especially next to rapids, so a set of nonverbal river signals using paddles or arms has been developed. Indicate you've received and understood a signal by repeating it back to the deliverer and passing it on to others who are behind you.

All Clear

One arm or paddle held vertically high above the head means it is safe to come ahead or keep coming. If using a paddle, the blade should be turned flat for maximum visibility. In the absence of other directions, proceed down the center of the river.

Direction

To signal direction (a preferred course through a rapid or around an obstruction), lower the vertical "all clear" by 45 degrees toward the side of the river with the preferred route. Never point toward the obstacle you wish to avoid.

Stop!

Arms outstretched horizontally mean a potential hazard is ahead. Stop in a safe place or pull to shore as quickly as possible. Wait for the "all clear" signal before proceeding or scout ahead.

Help! Emergency!
Signal an emergency with three long blasts on a whistle while waving a paddle, helmet, or life vest over your head. (A whistle is best carried on a lanyard attached to your life vest.) Whistles can be an effective signaling device if visual or verbal contact is not possible. A single whistle blast can be used to get people's attention. Whistles should only be used when necessary so they are taken seriously when they are heard. If you do not have a whistle in an emergency, use the visual signal alone. Assist the signaler as quickly as possible.

OK
Similar to scuba diving, place your hand on your head to indicate that you are OK. If someone gives you

this signal and you are OK, you should respond with the signal in return. If you are not OK, respond with a help signal.

STAYING ALERT
Rivers have objective and subjective hazards. Objective hazards include the river features we've already talked about—rocks, undercuts, strainers, and hydraulics. Subjective hazards are human factors, such as a breakdown in communication, and pose a unique challenge in a dynamic river environment. Accidents generally happen when an objective hazard overlaps with a subjective hazard, as when someone takes a swim in a gnarly rapid and her PFD is not fitted properly. The forces of a river's moving water compound the threat to life as a result of a mishap. Group members need to be clear about expectations. Something as simple as keeping everyone informed of the daily plan on the river or in which order boats will run a specific rapid is important.

Keep aware of your group and gear while you are on, in, or around rivers. The boaters in front of you might pull over because they see a potential hazard downstream. If you have been paying attention, you'll see them and can signal the boats behind you. Likewise, looking back upriver is important because a boat behind you may be signaling difficulty. Be aware of where other people in your group are.

Some people describe trip awareness as being aware of the trip in front of them, the trip behind them, and where they fit into the trip. Rivers with long, calm stretches can breed complacency in boaters, but you need to keep alert at all times on the river, not just while running rapids. Group management includes maintaining reasonable communication between boats, spacing boats properly for running rapids so you are close enough to back each other up but not so close that you get in each other's way, and placing specific boats in lead and sweep positions. (For example, you might have your friend in a highly maneuverable cataraft drop the rapid, and eddy out below the rapid as a spotter, to set safety. Her job is to help anyone who swims the rapid or has any other problem, and she needs to be immediately beneath the rapid, ready to row out and help a swimmer. You might have the boat with the first-aid kit, pullies, and certified first-aid guru go last in the sweep boat.) It is fine if group management strategies change as long as it's done actively and deliberately. Develop basic self-discipline at the team level and many major river problems will remain just minor incidents.

River
CROSSINGS

Timing is everything in some river rescues. Wading out to a person with an entrapped foot may be the simplest and fastest way to get to him. Once again, get proficient at crossing rivers long before you think you might need it.

Wading into or crossing a river safely takes careful planning, expertise, and deliberate execution. Travelers have to respect the river and its power. Preplanning, awareness, and managing risks are vital in outdoor travel; do not get complacent around moving water. No matter how many rivers you've crossed, you need to communicate, develop good crossing technique, and prepare intentionally and cautiously. When is it appropriate to consider a dry crossing like a highline or rope bridge? When is it better to wade? What conditions are too difficult to attempt a crossing? Judgment and decision-making about wading and river crossings are skills all river travelers need to develop.

EXPERTISE

NOLS students spend hours practicing basic river crossing techniques while being coached by seasoned instructors. This gives each person a feel for what conditions he can wade in and at what point he needs to use team techniques. It also helps in determining whether it's more appropriate to wade across a rapid or to swim. These few hours also give them real world experience that develops both the kinesthetic skills and judgment they will need for future river crossings. These exercises are done on a challenging and realistic section of a river with a good runout, with appropriate safety systems installed. Exposure to these safety systems teaches as much about the actual safety systems as it teaches about the contexts in which they are relevant. If you want to be a more versatile team member in a river rescue, you need to get good at river crossings long before you deal with an actual river rescue.

SCOUTING

All members should be comfortable with the location prior to committing to wading into the river. The trip schedule should not infringe upon solid decision-making. Make time to scout and avoid pressuring others or rushing into moving water before considering the group's options.

To determine the difficulty of crossing any drainage system, you need to consider many variables and what all those factors add up to. What hazards are present? Strainers—the trees, rock piles, or combinations of natural and human-made materials that allow water to pass through but trap solid objects—often appear harmless but should be regarded as threats to life. Getting a foot lodged on the riverbed floor is an emergency. The force of the water can push patients downstream, submerging their airways. Rocky bottoms that have sunken logs should be crossed with extreme care. Sandbars are often ideal places to cross with little chance of entrapment.

You also need to consider the gradient. Wider and flatter sections of river tend to be slower and shallower. Dark, fast water is typically deep. Use a stick to probe for depth when visibility is minimal.

Volume is another consideration. In thigh-deep water, most people cannot remain stable if the current is moving faster than 3 mph (5 km/h), which is roughly how fast a person can walk down an easy trail. Test the current's speed by tossing a stick into the main current and trying to keep pace with it while you walk down the riverbank. Keep in mind that water levels in snow-fed rivers typically rise as the day gets warmer and snow melts. Anticipate the diurnal low in the early morning after the melting process slows. Spring runoff also means more debris and trees washing down-stream. Listen for rocks tumbling across the riverbed, which could result in broken bones, loss of balance, and extended swims.

Use river features to your advantage. Eddy-hopping can be an effective way to wade across a wide streambed; teams can take breaks as they cross. Use upstream spotters to watch for debris and warn group members who are wading. Downstream, have two or more people prepared with a throw bag, a long stick, or other measure to aid in retrieving a swimmer from the river. Throwing a rope can add the danger of becoming entangled and should only be attempted by those trained in swiftwater rescue. Make sure the runout below the crossing is free of major rapids and hazards.

DRY-CROSSING TECHNIQUES

For a dry crossing, use any available land features, such as natural bridges, rocks, logjams, or trees, to keep dry while crossing. Always consider the consequences of an unsuccessful attempt: It could be as simple as getting wet socks or it could be as tragic as breaking a bone or even drowning. Dry crossings are usually only practical on a creek or small river.

Crossing surfaces are ideally stable, broad, and dry. Improve friction by sprinkling sand on slippery surfaces. Establishing a hand line at shoulder height can increase stability and confidence. Crossing over strainers can be a serious gamble because a slip into the water on the upstream side could be fatal. Logjams are essentially large strainers with questionable stability. They are best avoided if there is any doubt to their rigidity and ease of navigating.

WET-CROSSING TECHNIQUES

Practicing on land is an effective, low-exposure strategy for fine-tuning wet-crossing mechanics and builds confidence in what can be safely attempted on the river. As you become more comfortable, move to the water and attempt different techniques in a variety of currents and depths to determine the strengths and limitations of each crossing method.

The basic principle for all wet-crossing techniques is to create a moveable eddy with intentional foot placement, solid balance, and fluid weight transference. While taking a step, focus on the move and avoid looking at the destination. Once you have solid footing, then spot your target, offer feedback to others, or speak with folks on shore. While moving, however, focus 100 percent on the move so safety isn't jeopardized.

If a fall is inevitable, don't fight the process. Instead, just allow the fall and swim back to shore. Trying to arrest a fall can lead to foot entrapment. If the runout is shallow, use a defensive swim position by staying on your back with toes in the air. The default swim plan should be an aggressive swim back to shore to minimize time in water and exposure to hazards. Avoid standing up in moving water deeper than knee height. See the chapter on swimming skills for more instruction.

Individual Wading Technique

For deeper water, use a stick or paddle to establish a tripod support base. Keep legs wide, and face upstream. Stab the stick into the water and get solid purchase on the riverbed floor. Move one point of the tripod at a time, one foot at a time. Once your balance is set, relocate the stick for new purchase on the riverbed. Use caution—aim for small gains with each movement to avoid losing your balance.

Paired Technique

Two people can cross together safely by facing each other, one facing upstream and the other downstream, and holding on to each other. One person moves at a time. The upstream person (preferably the larger of the two) moves first, and then the downstream person steps into the first person's eddy. The downstream position is also good for a nervous group member; the upstream partner can give instructions and reassuring feedback. This method can be done even more securely with three people.

Group Techniques

Travelers wading as a group tend to be much more stable than those crossing alone. The pyramid, in-line crossing, and cross-pole techniques each have advantages and drawbacks. In all group techniques, communication is key.

The pyramid is best done with at least six people, a point person with two to three people in two lines behind her, forming a V that points into the current. The point person at the tip of the V should use a stick or pole for added support. Move sideways using small steps. Position nervous members in the middle of this configuration for protection.

For group in-line crossing, follow the individual technique described above, but add two to six people behind the first person. Place your hands on the shoulders of the person in front of you, preferably on the PFD; this provides pressure and stability to the entire line. Moving in small steps, the first person breaks the current and creates an eddy, and each member of the group then steps into the eddy.

Using a long branch, hiking pole, or paddle, three or more people can cross in a line perpendicular to the current, called cross-pole crossing. This method is surprisingly stable and is more effective with more people. If you slip, you can hold on to the pole while you regain your footing. Shorter people can be bridged across deep channels until they can touch again. With practice, this is effective in strong currents almost chest deep.

Wading is a powerful tool for the river rescuer. Practice wading alone and in groups to develop your physical talents and to develop an experience base. If you ever deal with a real river rescue, you probably won't remember reading this paragraph, but you probably will remember anything you have practiced. Like learning CPR, getting good at wading and other river rescue skills helps you back up your friends and other groups should you come around a bend when they need your help.

NOLS River Rescue
PHILOSOPHY

Before studying complex rescue techniques involving rope systems or pin extrications, you need a solid foundation in rescue philosophy. This increases awareness of basic priorities and will ultimately decrease the chances of becoming another patient in a real scenario.

RESCUE PRIORITIES
1st Priority: Rescuer Safety
2nd Priority: Group Safety
3rd Priority: Patient Rescue
4th Priority: Victim Recovery
5th Priority: Equipment Recovery

The first priority in all rescue situations is your own safety. Blindly and recklessly attempting to assist or save someone or a piece of equipment can often result in an unnecessary additional patient. Besides being tragic, this has huge operational costs to the first rescue by adding a second patient to the scenario. All too often in swiftwater, a would-be rescuer quickly becomes a patient himself after rushing into the river. As a rescuer, take a deep breath and evaluate the scene first.

The second priority is your group's safety. Back each other up and keep people calm, cool, collected, and rational. Before responding to a person in distress, make sure the rest of your group is out of harm's way. Avoid ending up with multiple patients by getting the rest of the group into a safe location.

The third priority, after stabilizing yourself and the group, is to rescue the patient. Rescue versus recovery is a difficult, but extremely important, distinction to make in this environment and is generally the difference between a patient and a victim. Any person in the river who is a candidate for a live rescue should be referred to as a patient. Anyone who has been heads-down (airway submersed) for greater than an hour should be considered unable to save and possibly referred to as a victim or recovery.

Victim recovery is the fourth priority in river rescue, after yourself, the group, and all patients are taken care of. Use firm, low-risk decision-making when recovering victims.

The fifth priority is equipment and gear recovery. Keep in mind that a lost oar, backpack, or boat is relatively trivial in comparison with that of a lost life. Only attempt to rescue gear and equipment if the risk of injury is low.

PRINCIPLES OF RIVER RESCUE
Brand-New Rapid
Approach all rapids as if it is your first time encountering them. Regardless of how many times you've established safety for a particular rapid, always be open-minded to new solutions and arrangements.

Manage Risk
Always consider deploying upstream spotters and downstream safety. Upstream spotters identify and warn the group of any debris or other boaters coming downstream into the rescue scenario. (A floating tree or raft that sweeps unknown into a rescue extrication could result in a devastating tragedy.) Others in the group can wait downstream with throw bags to help retrieve any group members that flush through.

K.I.S.S.

Keep it simple and safe. Lowest risk methods should always be your first consideration, while higher risk methods are being set up as alternatives. Avoid blindly relying on complex systems and mechanical devices. Systems theory tells us that doubling the number of components can quadruple the system's complexity and opportunities for errors. Simpler systems are generally more reliable systems.

Speech, Reach, Throw, Row, Go

This mnemonic device helps us remember the order of rescue techniques from lowest to highest risk. This particular order is for land-based rescues. With a boat-based rescue, it's often less risky to paddle to a swimmer than to throw him a rope, so for boat-based rescues the mnemonic would be Speech, Reach, Row, Throw, Go.

Speech: Often just quickly shouting to the patient, "Swim this way!" will have a dramatic effect on the outcome of the scenario. Communicating directly and immediately with the patient increases potential for a positive outcome.

Reach: Reach out with a stick or object to retrieve the patient.

Throw: Consider throwing a rope or flotation device.

Row: Paddle over to the patient and load him into your boat.

Go: Enter the river as a rescue swimmer in order to retrieve the patient.

Be Creative and Flexible

Less than forty years old, river rescue is a relatively new formal discipline, so innovative solutions are constantly being developed. Avoid narrow-mindedness and graciously encourage potential solutions from all group members, regardless of experience level. The best way to improve both your command of basic systems and your creativity is to practice.

Embrace Preplanning and Be Proactive

"Plan for the worst and hope for the best" is a great mantra when it comes to managing risk and getting trained in the appropriate techniques. Unfortunately, many who travel in and around rivers don't get training until after they experience a dangerous event. They respond to a difficult, sometimes tragic, situation, and then realize in the aftermath that they need more training. Go well beyond reading this book and get yourself trained in a two- or three-day swiftwater rescue course. Then practice, practice, practice.

Establish a STOP Command
Any group member on the river can use this command whenever he is not comfortable or when rescue or safety procedures need to be taken. Declare this as a group before embarking on any rescue situation.

Establish an Incident Commander
Whenever possible, there needs to be an incident commander (IC) who oversees the rescue operations. Ideally, the IC ensures effective communication and keeps the big picture in mind by staying hands-off. Discuss with your group ahead of time how this role will be assigned and what it entails so you can initiate an efficient rescue when it really matters.

RISK BENEFIT ANALYSIS
Determine the pros versus the cons of the rescue technique you are considering using. Decide whether the risk to yourself and your

group is worth the probability of a successful rescue. Historically there is a direct connection between heightened emotions and rescuer fatalities. Cease all rescue activities if it appears decisions are purely based on emotion.

RESCUE ANALYSIS

Prior to initiating any rescue, stop and analyze the rescue technique you are considering.

	Low Risk	High Risk
	The consequences of an unsuccessful attempt are relatively low.	The consequences of an unsuccessful attempt are relatively high.
High Probability		
There is a high probability of success with this technique.	**GO!** Give this technique a try.	Maybe. Try this technique or come up with a lower risk technique.
Low Probability		
There is a low probability of success with this technique.	Maybe. Try this technique or think of a different technique that has a higher probability of being successful.	**STOP!** Do not try this technique. Consider something else.

SCENE SIZE-UP

The foundation of sound decision-making is having a solid understanding of your present situation. Consider the following elements before rushing into a scene to help:

Danger

Is there an immediate risk of physical harm to you, fellow responders, bystanders, or the patient? How can that risk be minimized? If it's not safe to approach, then don't. You don't want another patient or a victim.

MOI (mechanism of injury)

What happened or is happening? Where was the patient last seen? What are the environmental hazards that could have contributed to the injury?

PPE (personal protective equipment)

Make sure you are wearing a PFD, helmet, and any other appropriate safety equipment.

Number of patients

Be aware that you may have other patients beyond the obvious screaming-front-and-center patient.

General impression
Is this a rescue or a recovery? What resources (people or equipment) do you have on hand that could help in this situation?

Probabilities
Consider the likeliest sequence of events and how your actions may affect those events. For example, if the patient is freed from a mid-stream entrapment prematurely, he could float right into a strainer 50 yards downstream; therefore, it would make sense to station a rescuer with a throw bag far above that strainer.

PLAN OF OPERATION
Using the information compiled from the scene size-up, you can make decisions and form a plan. Think ahead and create multiple plans because one of the probabilities may spoil your primary attack plan. Plan for the worst and hope for the best. If time allows, have an on-scene safety briefing to outline organization and management of the rescue.

Swimming
SKILLS

Paddlers always face the risk of capsizing or falling out of the craft and needing to swim to safety. If you find yourself swimming unexpectedly, the following basic guidelines can help you get to shore or back to your boat.

If you have to swim in a shallow, rocky river or in a rapid, stay in a defensive swimming position until you can swim aggressively to shore.

- Lie on your back with your feet downstream.
- Stay horizontal on the surface of the water by slightly arching your back.
- Keep your toes out of the water to avoid foot entrapment.
- If you see yourself going toward a hazard such as a large wave or hole, be assertive. Stay on your back and swim away from the object.

- If you encounter a rock, bend your knees and use your feet to push off the rock.
- Once you are out of the rapid, be assertive. Angle your head toward the closest, safest shore. Stay on your back, kick with your legs, and backstroke with your arms.
- Do not stand up until you are in shallow water or a calm eddy and less likely to trap your foot.

If you are in deeper water or are trying to reach a critical eddy, use an offensive or aggressive swimming position.

- Roll over on your stomach and use the crawl stroke.
- Keep your head out of the water in order to stay oriented to land and water features.
- Swim aggressively toward your intended target.
- Minimize knee and ankle injury by kicking with straight legs, keeping your legs from dangling too deep in the water.
- Again, do not stand up until you are less likely to trap your foot.

If you encounter large waves, try to swim away from them, since swimmers usually go through waves instead of floating over them. If you can't swim away from a wave in time, try

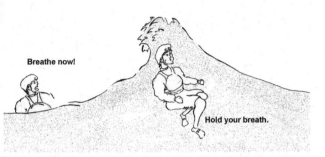

Swimming through a wave train requires patience and timing.

to catch a breath in its trough. Keep yourself oriented by looking around after you have taken a breath. In large waves, you are less likely to entrap your foot, so you can use an offensive swimming position.

If you find yourself in a hole, try to stay relaxed to conserve energy. The water in a hole moves in a circle, so it is easy to become disoriented. Swimmers sometimes flush straight through holes, but the current can also push you below the surface of the hole, toward the river bottom, and under the surface of the water until you wash out below the hole. If you are not flushed, try changing your shape so a different current might catch your body and pull you out of the hole. (Ball up or extend

When negotiating holes during a swim, balling up can minimize exposure and increase protection.

your arms and legs.) Another strategy is to swim toward the main current in order to catch a current near the river bottom to be flushed out of the hole.

If your boat flips, spilling you, your companions, and your gear, get to the upstream side of your boat and hold on to it or any gear for extra flotation. If you feel that continuing to hold on to your gear, boat, or paddle is compromising your safety, then let go and get on your back with your feet in front of you.

If you've just fallen out of your boat and you still have your paddle in hand, it may help

If you've just fallen out of your boat and you still have your paddle in hand, it may help to use the paddle to swim more efficiently.

to use the paddle to swim. Whether it's a canoe or kayak paddle, stroke with the paddle as you would if you were still in the boat and kick hard with your legs. This is a powerful technique, and done properly will result in a faster, more efficient swim as well as better visibility and access to air. Note, however, that it is very difficult to swim with a paddle if it isn't an active part of your stroke sequence.

As with all of these techniques, practice in low-stress training situations will give you the expertise you can depend on in more critical circumstances.

SWIFTWATER ENTRIES

As a last resort, rescuers sometimes need to get into the river quickly in order to attempt a rescue. Easing into the water may not be an option, and you may need to strategically jump into the main current. You may also want to jump in, in order to cross the first portion of a channel through the air rather than the water, preventing you from washing downstream too fast. Start at the most upstream portion of an eddy, and launch into the water so that you can see the patient. Practice extensively in a controlled environment in order to minimize injury.

Diving

Never dive into a river. Murky water, inconsistent river bottoms, and the dynamic nature of rivers make it difficult to accurately assess the depth of the river. Diving in shallow water is one of the leading causes of trauma in water-based accidents.

Lifeguard Jump

In very deep pools (greater than 6 feet deep), enter the water vertically with your eyes forward, arms out to the side, and legs spread forward and back. Upon impact slap your arms down while making a hard scissors kick to keep your face above water.

Hero Flop

Belly-flop like a skydiver might jump from a plane: back arched, arms out, legs back with feet trying to touch the back of the head. Upon impact with the water, slap your arms down to minimize how deep you go. Face upstream and angle your entry at 45 degrees to the current so that you can begin a proper ferry immediately and start strokes upon contact with the water.

The hero flop is one swiftwater entry technique that allows a rescuer to strategically enter the main current to attempt a rescue.

Throw Bags and
ROPE HANDLING

THROW BAGS

Throw bags are rescue devices that all boaters must be proficient at using and need to carry on rivers. They are simple in design, consisting of a nylon, self-draining bag with 30 to 80 feet of rope stacked inside. They enable a rescuer to extend her reach using a rope, allowing the swimmer, in some situations, to grab the rope and be pulled to shore. If someone throws you a throw bag while you are swimming, grab the rope itself and not the bag. If the rope lands several feet away from you, be assertive and aggressively swim to it. Once you grab the rope, place it over your upstream shoulder, holding on to it with both hands, so that your body assumes the correct ferry angle and you are able to breathe more easily. Keep your hands close to your chest, your face up, and your feet downstream. Do not tie or wrap the rope around any part of

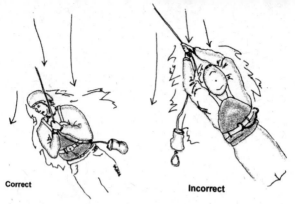

Correct

Incorrect

Holding onto a rope in a current can be extremely difficult. Practice techniques that maximize strength while maintaining an airway.

your body. Once the rescuer has pulled you to a safe place, you can let go of the rope. If you feel that you are being put in greater jeopardy by continuing to hold on to the rope, let go.

Familiarize yourself with the design of throw bags and the different types and sizes of rope. Practice throwing and receiving the rope before your trip. Knowing how to efficiently use a throw bag is the foundation for all advanced rescue skills. Be creative and fashion well-managed scenarios for practice.

Be comfortable throwing overhand, under-hand, and sidearm with both arms at moving targets. Practice on dry land and in the water.

Practice your throw bag technique before *embarking on your river trip.*

Experiment with wading out to waist level and making the same attempts.

Assess the terrain of the riverbank to find the best spot to throw from. A swimmer rescued by a rope will ideally swing like a pendulum into a safe eddy, not through dangerous obstacles or rapids. Also consider what might happen if the rescuer is pulled off balance and into the river.

After you throw the bag, you may need to make a second attempt if you made an unsuccessful toss, the swimmer missed the rope, or an additional swimmer came through the rapid. You can use the coil method or the full-bag-of-water method to make a quick retrieval and throw a second time.

The coil method allows you to gather and throw only what you need so you don't have too much rope in the water, which can be hazardous. Make smooth, even coils about 12 to 18 inches in diameter in your throwing hand. Throw the coils with a smooth and firm hand rather than fast and jerky.

For the full-bag-of-water method, step on the end of the rope after the first attempt, and quickly stack the rope at your feet as you pull in the bag. When the bag arrives at shore, it will be full of water and ready for a fast second toss.

Getting into a solid, athletic position after throwing a rope is one of the most effective ways to prevent you from getting pulled into the river or injured. Bend your knees and get your center of gravity low. Brace yourself on natural features such as rocks and roots. Have a group member back you up by grabbing your PFD lapels. If you can't hold the rope without getting pulled into the river, you should not throw it to the patient.

Use friction bends around trees and rocks to lessen the load considerably: Simply walk the taut line around a solid, inanimate object to minimize force on your body.

A second rescuer can help retrieve a swimmer who has hold of the line by *vectoring* the line. Use your hand or clip a sling to the line, and walk down the shoreline toward the swimmer. Pulling sideways like this shortens the retrieval distance and can also help avoid swinging through obstacles.

ROPE HANDLING: KNOT TYING

Fundamental knot-tying skills are extremely helpful in a rescue when seconds count. You should be able to tie the following knots on the spot in fewer than sixty seconds. Practice tying smooth and flawless knots until they become second nature—the emotions and distractions of a live rescue can become overwhelming. Every minute counts in a rescue, and you don't want to struggle to tie one of these knots.

Water Knot

The water knot is the best knot for joining two ends of 1-inch tubular webbing. It is an overhand follow-through with 2 to 3 inches of tail on either end of the dressed knot.

Figure Eight Follow-Through

This knot is used to join two ends of rope together. You can tie prusik loops with this knot, eliminating the need for the more traditional, but often harder to tie, double fisherman's knot.

The Bowline

The bowline is an excellent choice for securing a boat to shore or a throw bag to a canoe's bow/stern loop.

Improved Prusik Hitch

This is a friction knot used in many mechanical advantage systems. The third wrap is what makes this improved.

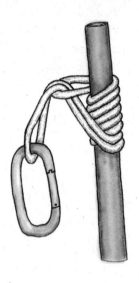

The Klemheist

The klemheist is an alternative choice for the the improved prusik hitch. Different than the prusik hitch, the klemheist can only be loaded in one direction. Advantages are that it can be effectively tied with both rope or 1" tubular webbing. You can add more friction with more wraps. This is helpful when the hitch is wet and works great with 1" tubular webbing. It is very easy to tie and untie.

Clove Hitch

The clove hitch is great for anchor systems.

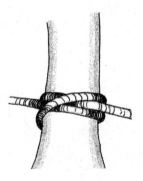

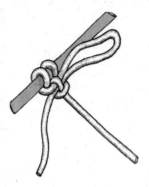

The Thief Hitch

The thief hitch has excellent applications in canoe rescue. It makes a relatively secure knot, is simple to tie, and most important, is quick to release.

The Mountaineers Coil & the Butterfly Coil

There are numerous ways in which to coil a rope for storage and for throwing. Two that are ideal for use on the river are the mountaineer's coil (right) and the butterfly coil (left).

LIMITED-SLIP GIRTH HITCH

The limited-slip girth hitch is an advanced hitch designed to secure a patient by the wrist without damaging tissue. It stabilizes a patient trapped in an undercut rock or strainer but ideally isn't used to extract the patient. Remember basic first aid and the ABCs (airway, breathing, circulation). Stabilizing the patient's airway and breathing are the first priorities, and you can achieve this by pulling with enough force to keep the patient's head and airway above water. Be mindful of not pulling with so much force that the patient's shoulder pops out of joint. On the other hand, if she is about to drown because her airway is submersed, consider pulling on anything possible to get her air—even if this means dislocating a shoulder.

The limited-slip girth hitch is simply a girth hitch on top of another girth hitch, which reduces the amount it can cinch. Webbing is preferable, as it tends to cut into the skin less than rope, but in an emergency either will do fine. When seconds count, use a regular girth hitch or any other knot that will keep the patient's airway open. The limited-slip girth hitch is preferable because it limits the pain and permanent tissue damage that will result if it is a prolonged extraction. A more comfortable patient has more energy reserves and can communicate more effectively. To be prepared for such an event, keep a flip-line made of webbing tied in a loop double-wrapped around your waist. This can double as an anchor piece as well.

Tying the Limited-Slip Girth Hitch

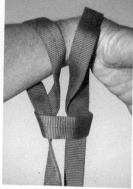

Left: Grab the line with both hands, and twist loops in each hand in opposite directions with two full twists per loop. **Right:** Put the two loops together and slip over the patient's hand.

ROPE FERRIES

Ferrying a rope across the river can be used for several applications, including stabilizing and extrication lines, telfer lowers, or a wading assist line. In many watersheds there is often too great a distance for this skill to be of much use. However, there are rapids, constrictions, midstream eddies, and channels created by islands where ferrying a line can be very effective. Knowing how to ferry a rope can make all the difference in an emergency, and it takes considerable practice and awareness to become proficient.

A kayak or canoe is typically the fastest, most efficient way to ferry a rope. The next best boat is a paddle raft. If a craft isn't available, then a wading team may have to take the rope across.

The surface area of a ⅜-inch rope extending 50 feet across a river is about 1.6 square feet. This can cause considerable drag, so discuss what the person on shore can do to eliminate drag (hold the rope high, skip it upstream, feed out adequate slack). Use the current to your advantage by having the ferrying boat start upstream of the person holding the line to create a pendulum effect to the target area on the opposing shore. Emphasize speed and finesse. Take the extra time to make the first attempt successful.

When possible have another rescuer waiting on the opposite shore to grab the line from the ferrying craft. It can be difficult for the ferrying paddler to get out of the boat with the line.

The ideal way to carry a rope is on a rescue PFD with a releasable harness. Holding it with one hand in a releasable grip is another option. Avoid using your teeth because you could injure your teeth, gums, mouth, or face when the line goes taut.

Weigh the benefits and disadvantages of a messenger line, a long, thin, strong piece of string that is ferried across the river before the rope. The messenger line causes less drag, and the stronger rope is then attached to the end of it and pulled across. Messenger lines can be difficult to deal with, turning into a pile of tangled spaghetti when you attempt to pay them out. When seconds count, it is sometimes better to just use a heavy line to begin with and take every precaution to make the first attempt successful.

Recognize some of the biggest concerns when ferrying a line.

Releasability: Can I let go of this rope if I need to? Will it get caught up and create another hazard if I do?

Obstructions: Could the rope get snagged on something while ferrying it across?

Missing your route: What do I do if it takes longer than I anticipate to get the rope across and I end up much farther downstream?

SWIMMING A LINE ACROSS THE RIVER

You may not have time to retrieve a boat for a rope ferry if the patient's airway is submersed. Be sure to start way upstream of your target to account for rope drag, which will swing you like a pendulum downstream as you swim to the other side. Practicing this skill will help you realize how difficult rescues can be and make you more cautious when sizing up a rapid. Choose narrow channels to practice this skill or simply target a midstream eddy.

Rescuing Swimmers, BOATS, AND GEAR

On many rivers, there can be a large amount of recovery time between rapids during a rescue. Don't let this make you complacent. During a real-life scenario when it matters most, boaters should be able to react appropriately and quickly. Group members should inspire each other to take advantage of each rescue as an opportunity to become a more efficient rescuer. Try not to use the mile of runout below a rapid simply because it is available. Instead, strive to recover the swimmer, boat, or gear expeditiously and proficiently while maintaining respect for the river.

All paddlers should gain proficiency in self-rescue. Occasionally a group can hold off on recovering a swimmer or equipment as a learning experience. Encourage the novice paddlers in the group to hold on to their gear while swimming. If the wave train is reasonable and the swimmer is comfortable, support him to make the ferry swim with boat and paddle. Remember that ferries are executed by swimming upstream at a 45-degree angle in relationship to the current. Coach him to abandon gear when approaching obstructions or heavy water, but positively reinforce attempts to hold on to equipment. He will not always have the safety net of a nearby companion. Kayakers need to ensure their stern air bags are full with their belongings secure inside.

GENERAL RULES FOR RESCUING SWIMMERS & EQUIPMENT

- Always communicate with the patient and other rescuers.
- Chase people first, gear second.
- When possible, split the load between two rescuers: one retrieve the swimmer and one go after gear. Be sure to communicate this even if eye contact is difficult.
- Think about what is coming next and anticipate any problems.
- Avoid clipping into equipment or people unless you have ample time for release.

SWIMMER RECOVERY

No matter what your craft, paddle alongside the swimmer and coach him to shore. Encourage him to hold on to his gear when appropriate.

In a kayak, ask the swimmer to grab your stern grab loops and kick as you paddle. Newer designs have security loops directly behind the cockpit that allow a swimmer to get farther out of the water and into a more comfortable kicking position, but this can also throw off weight distribution.

Have the swimmer face you while grabbing the bow loop and wrapping his legs around the bow of the kayak. This allows you to plow the swimmer to shore while also maintaining eye contact with him.

In a raft, extend a T-grip to reach a swimmer. Also use T-grip to T-grip connections. Grab the swimmer's PFD while facing him. On the count of three, lean back and pull him into the raft almost on top of you.

Encourage the crew to practice throw bag tosses and to catch challenging eddies.

With canoeists, assist the tired and cold swimmer by coaching her to hold the stern grab loop and paddle her to shore.

KAYAK PADDLE RECOVERY

To recover a group member's kayak paddle that is floating in the current, consider the following options: Kayak up to the paddle, throw the paddle, and chase it until it reaches an eddy, a raft, or lands on shore. If the paddler's hands are large enough, the paddles can double up and be paddled to shore. Or you can clip into the shaft of the paddle with a carabiner and tow system. If you do not have a paddle carabiner, consider clipping around the paddle shaft back onto the tether as in a girth hitch.

KAYAK RECOVERY

To recover an empty kayak that is floating in the river, consider the following options as you approach in your kayak: For the snow plow, hook the cockpit with the bow of your boat and then plow the capsized kayak to shore. Push on the upstream end of the boat, opposite from the eddy you are aiming for, in order to set a ferry angle.

Alternately, use a tether system attached to a rescue PFD to tow the kayak to shore.

Regardless of the method you use, try to keep the kayak upside down, so the air pocket inside the boat stays intact while you tow or plow it to shore. Refrain from uprighting the kayak unless it is taking on water.

If it is taking on water, turn it over and begin plowing into the cockpit.

If you need to, pull the kayak over your deck and rock it side to side until the water drains out. Then flip it upright onto the surface of the water and tow it or push and chase it until you reach the shore.

Consider using two rescuers, side by side, working together to push the boat toward an eddy. Communication is key in maintaining the ferry angle and targeting on shore or an eddy.

PADDLE RAFT RECOVERY

Practice capsize drills before embarking on a paddle raft trip. If a paddle raft flips with no rescuers nearby, the boaters need to be self-sufficient. While standing on top of the upside-down raft, clip a throw rope or webbing onto a D-ring or the perimeter line of the raft in the middle on one of the sides of the raft. Pull on this line as you stand on the opposite side and lean back. Your body weight should be enough to flip the raft back over. If not, recruit extra people until you have enough strength and weight to pull the raft back over. Be extra cautious in ensuring this recovery technique is performed in deep water so no injuries occur.

OAR RAFT RECOVERY

Discussing preplanning methods for recovery of a flipped oar raft could mean the difference between a quick, efficient recovery and one that lasts several miles. It's easy to become entangled, entrapped, or injured by an upside-down oar raft, so discuss strategy as a team prior to running any rapids where this hazard is present.

Rigging to Chase

Oar rafts can weigh over a ton. Combine this with the pressures of the current, and there will be considerable strain on your system if you attempt to tow an upside-down oar raft with your own raft. Consider always using Spectra throw bags or static lines with high breaking strengths when rigging to chase. All oar rafts in the fleet should be rigged this way, and you should consider running the rapids close to one another when flipping potential is high. This will shorten the chase dramatically.

To set up for rigging to chase: Run the working end of the throw bag line (with no knots in it) through the center D-ring in the bow of the raft and back toward the frame bar in front of the rower. Wrap the frame bar in front of the rower with a single sling and carabiner. Tie the working end of the throw bag to this carabiner with a releasable clove hitch. Clip the bag close to the bow D-ring and toss it to people on top of the flipped oar rig. Instruct them to clip it into one of their D-rings. The rescuing raft can now pull for an eddy and swing the flipped boat to shore.

By rigging to chase you also rig to flip. This means you are ready to chase flipped rafts and at the same time are ready to be chased should your raft flip. When you clip the throw bag for the rigging-to-chase system close to the bow D-ring, the rope is then available for swimmers, members of the paddle raft, or another oar raft.

Secure all baggage and items to the raft so that everything stays in place in the event of a flip. Be careful with pockets in the cargo area where feet can become entrapped.

Consider packing your rescue kit in an independent dry bag at the bow or stern for easy retrieval in case the boat flips and then becomes stuck on rocks.

A paddle raft can ram and plow a flipped oar rig toward shore fairly effectively as long as the paddlers paddle well together and know the flipped boat's present ferry angle. Those on the paddle raft can also assist in rigging to chase by timing their landing on shore to coincide with the towing raft's proximity to shore and the target eddy. They can then make a throw bag toss to the towing raft and wrap their end of the rope around a tree or rock to swing both oar rafts to shore. Once the tensionless anchor is set, other paddle raft members can then vector-pull the rope to shore.

CANOE RECOVERY
Self-Rescue
Prerig the canoe in one of two ways:

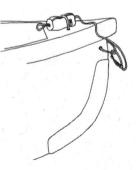

1. Rig your canoe with a throw bag tied to the stern with a bowline and have the throw bag either under the painter bungee or placed

loose in the boat with the line stacked neatly in the bag and the drawstring tight (see illustration on previous page).

2. Feed the working end of the throw line through the stern grab loop and tie a thief hitch to the grab handle or a thwart, making sure the line is clear from the body (you can run this under the seat to keep it clear if going to the thwart). This option sets the canoe up for not only self-rescue but also the boat-assisted rescue described later in this section (see illustration).

If your canoe capsizes, swim over to the throw rope, and with it still tied to the canoe,

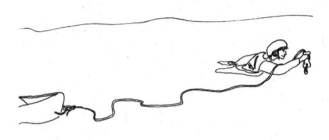

swim the bag (and remaining rope) back to
shore. Swim hard slightly downstream toward
shore (see illustration above). Ideally you will
get to shore before the rope becomes taut. Find
a natural anchor such as a tree or rock and
wrap the rope around it. Keeping your hands
and fingers clear of the line, the natural anchor
will now assume the force of the load and
swing the canoe to shore.

If you are swimming in a rock garden,
align the boat with the current to slip between
obstacles. Once you reach a clear section, begin
swimming the throw rope back to shore as
described above.

Use the Capistrano flip to turn over a capsized canoe. Paddlers swim under the capsized
canoe and in unison scissors kick to push it
above the surface and roll it into the air with
less water in it.

To empty a canoe that has taken on water, try the shakeout technique to eliminate excess water. Paddlers keep the swamped boat upright in the water while one person pushes down on an end of the canoe while also pushing the boat forward. The end must lift before the water flows back in. An alternative is to push down and away on one side and then pull up on the gunwale before water flows back in.

Boat-Assisted Towing Rescue

Use the towing method when dealing with loaded expedition canoes, especially in wide continuous rivers. Consider the short line and the long line methods.

Short-Line Tow

Short Line: Grab the painter line from either the bow or stern of the capsized boat, whichever is most accessible. Run this line through the stern grab loop of the rescuing canoe, under the seat, and then secure it to the thwart with a thief hitch. This is a releasable setup in case the rescuer needs to detach from the swamped canoe quickly. This short line method is good for long distance tows in moving current as well as slow-moving water, and keeping the capsized boat close to the rescuer boat makes it significantly easier to tow than if it is far away in the water at the end of a long line. If possible, rolling the canoe in the water, to be towed upright, makes the towing much easier, but this can be tricky and takes practice.

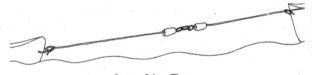

Long-Line Tow

Long Line: This method works great for high-volume, fast-moving water where the river is narrow enough to get to shore before the line tensions. It requires prerigging canoes with throw bags for rescue prior to launching that day, and you can do this with one throw bag or two.

One Throw Bag: Feed the working end of the throw line through the grab loop and thief hitch it to a thwart. Have the bag end of the throw line accessible with a carabiner on the end of the bag. This line can be clipped to the grab loop of the capsized boat for assisted tow recovery.

Two Throw Bags: Prerig all canoes in your party to have a throw bag as their stern painter. It should be secured to the canoe using a bowline on the grab loop. Using a second throw bag, the rescuing canoe sets up the same as the one-throw-bag method. Locating the stern, clip the loop on the capsized throw bag and begin towing. This method allows for more line length to get to shore before the heavy load impedes progress. The strategy of the long line method is not to tow the capsized loaded boat, but rather to pendulum belay the boat to shore before the throw line tensions.

For a boat-over-boat rescue, lift the capsized boat over the gunwales of the rescue boat. Swimmers should help when possible. Roll the empty boat upright and slide it back into the water. Stabilize the boat while swimmers reenter it.

Assist a swimmer performing a self-rescue by offering him your towline.

You can bump or plow the boat as you tow the swimmer.

If you are on shore, throw a bag to a swimmer holding onto the canoe and vector-pull to get him to shore faster.

Mechanical Advantage
AND ANCHOR
SYSTEMS

Seasoned paddlers should be able to build a solid anchor and set up a mechanical advantage system in a few minutes without supervision. Ideally, group members would always be available to double-check one another, but in reality, you cannot be too dependent on each other. Become confident in your rope systems.

KEY CONSIDERATIONS FOR ALL SYSTEMS

- Designate a leader, a rescue boater, upstream spotters, and downstream safety.
- All rescuers must wear helmets and PFDs and have knives readily available.
- To lessen friction, pulleys are always better than carabiners for changes of direction.
- Secure an object (such as an extra PFD) to any haul line in the system that could break and fly back toward rescuers. Ropes with

carabiners attached to them have the potential of becoming deadly projectiles should they break free from their anchors. For example, a haul line could be attached to a D-ring on a raft, and that D-ring's glue patch could break free from the raft and hurl the line and D-ring toward the rescuers. Simply clip the PFD or other soft, dead weight object directly to the haul line as close to the potential breaking point as possible.

- Evaluate river hazards and currents in terms of access to the boat and risk management.
- Plan first and make sure everyone understands his role and the signals.

MECHANICAL ADVANTAGE SYSTEMS

Strong Arm Technique: This should always be one of your first considerations. Secure a line to the boat and have your entire group pull on it. If enough people are available, put them to work rather than building a complex, time-consuming system. If twelve people cannot pull the boat out of the pinned situation, then a mechanical advantage system can't do much more before components of the system begin to fail.

For a 2:1 vector pull, secure one line from the boat directly to an anchor either by itself or on a 3:1 (or other mechanical advantage system). Then place your pulling power on a second line that is clipped or fixed to the first line. This not only comes close to doubling your efforts but also offers the benefit of a new direction of pull. Ideally you want to pull on a 45-degree angle to the current pinning the boat, and a vector pull can be the most effective way of achieving this angle.

The 3:1 Z-drag (see illustration) is the classic system and one that all boaters should be able to build while blindfolded. It gives a 3:1 mechanical advantage and can be set up quickly with minimal equipment.

Attach the haul line to the pinned boat. Determine the ideal angle of pull and locate an anchor point. Attach a pulley to the anchor. Run the haul line from the pinned boat through the anchor pulley. Attach a second pulley (the traveling pulley) to the haul line with a prusik. Run the haul line through the traveling pulley and back to shore.

Most adults can pull at least 50 percent of their weight, if not more, so it is reasonable and prudent to never create more than a 12:1 advantage. (That is, no more than four people should pull on a 3:1.) Aside from reaching a point of diminishing returns with elaborate mechanical advantage arrangements, a system greater than 12:1 has the dangerous potential of equipment failure. Tests performed in NOLS river rescue training seminars on 11 mm static lines show that 7 mm prusik knots slip and burn between 750 and 1,300 pounds. Once slipping occurs, cease pulling because the potential of the system has been maxed out and something is about to fail. If the boat is still stuck, a better solution is to change attachment points or the angle of pull, not increase mechanical advantage. Many fire departments have standard operating procedures that prohibit the safety officer from allowing a system to be greater than 8:1. This is to err on the conservative side but illustrates that 12:1 is at the high end of acceptable advantage.

ANCHOR BUILDING SYSTEMS

Building self-equalizing or load-distributing anchors is an essential skill that coincides well with the dynamics of an ever-changing river environment. The disadvantage is that if one of the points in the anchor fails, the other points are shock-loaded as the slack is taken out. The most effective placement for a load-distributing anchor is on the boat itself, as it will often shift many times before releasing.

Alternately, load-sharing distributes the load evenly between anchor points and will not allow for shock loading. But the load is shared only in one direction, so if the haul line moves, then one anchor point will be supporting more or all of the weight.

Another option is to wrap a tree or boulder twice and then clip the tail back on to itself with a carabiner for a tensionless anchor. Deadman anchors buried in sandy beaches are also worth considering, whereas spikes driven into beaches generally can't hold rescue loads.

Determining and communicating the best locations for point of attachment in the middle of a pin can be difficult with the roar of the river. Discuss the rigging methods and points of attachment on the boat prior to heading into the field. A cradle or multiple tie-off points are better than using a single attachment point. Points for consideration on various crafts include (in order of general strength):

Raft: Perimeter-tube, thwarts, frames, D-rings

Canoe: Wrap the entire boat or thwarts close to their attachment (Avoid attaching to seats as they could shatter when pulled upon.)

Kayak: Wrap the entire boat, security bars, seat, and/or grab loops

TENSIONED ZIP LINES

Suppose your raft is pinned in the middle of the river with people in it and the sun is setting. This is not necessarily a life-threatening situation, but you certainly don't want to spend the night on the raft when you can instead deal with it in the morning. Using a zip line, you can safely transport people back to land. If you have a scared group member, a practiced paddler can cross the zip line with that person to offer him support.

A zip line allows a controlled crossing of water that is too deep or fast for wading. Angle the line across the current with the direction of travel downstream. A swimmer clips into the line using a webbing loop and carabiner and holds on, letting the river do the work. Zip lines are most often used to get a group off a pinned raft.

- Establish rope at a 45-degree angle to the current (not to the riverbanks).
- Anchor the upstream end of the rope securely. You may need a hauling system (a 3:1 or another alternative) on the shore end of the rope to create enough tension.
- Put the sling over your upstream shoulder to set the ferry angle. Make sure nothing (such as a chest-mounted knife) is in the way of a release.
- Establish downstream safety and upstream spotters.

TELFER LOWER

The telfer lower is an excellent technique for reaching a patient, boat, or piece of equipment, but it does take considerable time and commu-

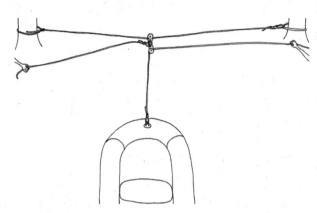

A telfer lower is set up to control the move of a rescuer from an upstream position to a downstream position to aid retrieving a patient or piece of gear.

nication to set up safely. Named after a *telferage*, a cable car system like a ski gondola, it is essentially a belay/rappel system used to control the lowering of a craft from an upstream position to a position downstream just above a patient or piece of equipment. The telfer lower may be the best solution for recovering a person or boat from an undercut or pin. Learning and applying the system also encourages greater care when navigating near undercuts with novices in your boat. When scouting rapids with entrapment potential, be sure to preplan your sequence of actions in the event that someone becomes entrapped. A telfer lower may not be your first choice, but it should be one alternative. Even with a group of several river professionals, telfer lowers often take hours to set up, practice, and break down. The telfer lower should be learned in a river rescue course and is briefly explained here to illustrate the possibilities.

- Telfer lowers can be performed with rafts, kayaks, and canoes. Arrange and secure kayaks and canoes in groups of three to create a wider base of support and greater stability.
- Establish downstream safety and upstream spotters.

PIN EXTRICATIONS
Boat-Pinning Mechanisms

River runners should be familiar with the general ways in which a boat becomes pinned or broached. You should have a solid understanding of what the following terms mean: center pins, end-to-end pins, vertical pins, and pinch pins. By becoming familiar with the arrangement of particular pins, you can be far more efficient in their extractions.

A *center pin* occurs when a boat sweeps sideways onto a rock or obstruction. The buildup of current on the boat results in the bow and stern wrapping around the rock.

The bow and stern of the boat both get stuck on two different rocks in the *end-to-end pin*. The boat then collapses in the center where there is the most force and least amount of support.

Pinch pins occur when one end of the boat lodges between two or more rocks and the current collapses the boat downstream.

Vertical pins occur when a boat goes over a steep but shallow ledge system. If it goes over bow first, the bow dives deep into the water and gets wedged on the riverbed floor. The paddler can easily become entrapped by the force of the water. Vertical pins usually occur with canoes or kayaks and not as often with rafts.

Strong-Arm Techniques

Keep it simple. If you can reach the boat or swim safely to it, often a solid tug or push will alleviate the pin. Creative pushing, pulling, and jarring have unpinned many boats. Take a moment to look around and ask yourself a few questions. Where is most of the water holding the boat? Where should I push and in what direction? Can I use the river's power to my advantage?

Determining Direction of Pull
The direction of pull should be 45 degrees to the current pinning the boat. This requires the rescuer to study the pin carefully to determine exactly which current has the most influence on the pin. It may take some creativity to achieve such an angle based on your present surroundings.

Wrapping the Boat for Rotational Release
Use the strength of the river to your advantage when pulling on a pinned boat. You can wrap canoes, rafts, and kayaks with a haul line so that they rotate and dump water out as force is applied. Pulling the submerged edge directly back up means working directly against the current. Instead, wrap the boat with a haul line so it rolls upstream, using the current to empty the boat of water and free it from the pin.

Special Considerations for Rafts
When rafts are severely pinned and you have tried every method to relieve the boat, you

can try to release some air out of the perimeter tubes. You may have to deflate all of them to free the boat. This should be used as a last resort, however, as an inflated boat tends to float much better after releasing from a pin than a deflated one, and you want to consider the runout below the pin. You also run the risk of getting water in the tubes, which can be a real hassle to extract. Generally, inflated tubes work to your favor, as they want to come to the surface, and you just need to make that an option for them. Releasing air reduces the bucket effect of the current pouring into the raft's passenger compartments. If the floor is laced in, you can cut it to reduce this same effect. Glued-in floors can also be cut but are expensive and laborious to repair.

A paddle raft can become pinned in the middle of the river, where running ropes to shore may be unreasonable, dangerous, or time-consuming. Consider setting up a 3:1 Z-drag inside the raft off opposing D-rings in the bow and the stern to relieve the pin. This is a reason why all boaters should carry pin kits and may also work with some canoe pins.

Special Considerations for Kayaks

Newer kayaks have broach loops in front of and behind the cockpit. These are strategic points of contact that relieve pressure off the legs and release a patient during a pin. Broach loops made of tubular webbing are strong when new, but they tend to wear out quickly in the sand and sun. Metal attachment points offer more strength and reliability in the long term of the boat's life.

As an extreme measure, a pinned kayak may be cut or sawed open, often behind the cockpit. A knife will work, but it is extremely slow and tedious. A small folding saw makes quick work of most plastics and should be as accessible as the rest of your pin kit. Take special care not to injure the patient. If you need to cut in the bow of the boat feel around underwater to determine where the patient's legs are in relation to the outfitting. As a general rule, cutting and relieving the stern is the fastest, safest, most efficient method. Begin at the rear of the cockpit inside the coaming. Make a relief cut at least 8 inches long down the side toward the hull of the boat. When possible, make an identical cut on the opposite side to allow the stern to peel away.

Entrapment and
UNCONSCIOUS
PATIENTS

Dealing with entrapment and unconscious patients is one of the scariest scenarios imaginable on a river trip. The right number of rescuers is the minimum needed to do the job. Group members not directly involved with an extraction should work elsewhere, managing the group and delegating other group members as upstream spotters and downstream safety. Remaining group members should not overwhelm a rescue scene with their presence but anticipate that they may be called upon to add more muscle power to the scene. It often makes sense to evacuate uninjured paddlers first to give the rescuers more room to work. Although the material in this section can be scary, it is important to understand the possible outcomes and how to positively impact your situation if you become entrapped.

GENERAL RULES FOR ENTRAPPED PATIENTS

- Offer continuous support.
- Stabilize first, then extricate.
- Look at the big picture.

PROBABLE CAUSES FOR ENTRAPMENT

- Foot entrapment
- Undercuts or pin rocks
- Outfitting, apparel, or shoes

HEADS-UP AND HEADS-DOWN PATIENTS

In a heads-up pin, you have some time, but don't take it for granted. Stabilize the patient's position as soon as possible before deciding on an extraction technique. If her kayak skirt is sealed, tell her to keep it that way until you arrive. As a general rule, secure as many attachment points to both boat and paddler as soon as possible before determining direction of pull. That way, if the boat shifts unexpectedly, you don't have to worry about accessing those points. Avoid complacency even in relatively straightforward situations. Read your patient's state of mind and talk to her constantly. Tell her what you are going to do, not to panic, and that you are going to help, which boosts morale. Sometimes you can take a cool, calm, collected approach, and other times you must be very aggressive in your speech. Your job may be as simple as holding her head above water until help arrives.

A heads-down pinning is a life-or-death matter. In this case, the imminent risk of death justifies extreme measures, even though they will probably cause injury. It's reasonable to tie a rope to a patient's arm or leg while trying to pull her free. Try to pull a paddler out the way she went in from upstream rather than pulling with the current, which can make the entrapment worse. The heads-down patient has no airway, so consider giving rescue breaths underwater—this person needs oxygen immediately.

DEALING WITH FOOT ENTRAPMENT
The Stabilization Line
The stabilization line secures the airway and gives timely support.

Begin downstream of the patient, establishing a rope across the channel. The distance between the two rescuers should be as short as possible. Wading may be effective in reaching a shoal on the other side of patient. You may need two or three ropes clipped together. Rocks are not that helpful in weighting down the rope. Keep the rope out of the patient's reach until both belayers are ready, or a rescuer could be unexpectedly pulled in.

The belayers then move upstream and try to create a 90-degree bend in the rope around the patient. The rope should rest under the arms and across the chest of the patient, alleviating stress.

Be sure the belayers pull evenly so the patient doesn't experience the results of a tug-of-war. If you apply too much force, the rope will go up over the head of the patient, who will fall facedown again. The main objective of the stabilization line is to open and secure the patient's airway. Watch closely and coach the patient to try to free himself.

The Snag Line

Use the snag line to release a trapped foot after the patient is stabilized.

Perform this the same way as the stabilization line, but the target for contact with the patient is low on the leg that is entrapped. Do not bother weighting down this line, as it will find its own way down the leg and the patient can help work the rope down her leg.

Have a strong swimmer downstream ready to retrieve an exhausted patient. Once the patient is freed, have one side pull the line in and the other pay rope out to get the patient to shore. Another option is to simply have the rescuer on one side let go of the rope to allow the swimmer to pendulum to the opposite shore.

Patient Energy Conservation Techniques
Entrapped patients often flail wildly, expending all their energy in a matter of seconds. Instead, find a secure, static position to breathe in. Even with a full curtain of water pouring over your head, you can still position your face to breathe. Discover and create ways to prop yourself up to breathe without exhausting yourself, for example placing your arms on your knee and propping your upper body in a stable position or swimming to the top for air, taking a deep breath, and then going face down again until you need another breath.

DEALING WITH UNCONSCIOUS PATIENTS

In a Kayak

Pull alongside the capsized kayak in a parallel position, place one hand on the hull closest to you, and place the other hand on the opposite side. Then in an opposing push-pull motion, upright the kayak and open the patient's airway.

If you can't barrel roll the patient's boat as described above, you may need to exit your boat, remove the patient from his boat, and swim for shore.

In the Water

In heavy rapids or to avoid hazards such as undercuts, you may have to prioritize retrieving the patient over opening his airway. By clipping in with a rescue harness, you are free to paddle the patient to shore, where you can administer first aid. Weave the carabiner of the tether through the lapels of the PFD and then back onto itself. This helps clear and maintain an open airway.

You can try pulling the patient onto the deck of your kayak. This is obviously difficult in little boats, but it may prove effective while waiting for raft support.

In some situations, you may want to bail out of your boat and swim the patient to shore.

If you are with another kayaker, orient the kayaks on either side of the patient. Establish the airway and wait for raft support.

Final Thoughts

After reading this book you may be asking yourself, Where do I go from here? How well would I respond in an emergency on the river? Successful rescues are a result of infinite variables, but a few major factors can be attributed to many victories:

Training
Be sure to take a two- or three-day swiftwater rescue course. Try to take one designed for boaters who do boat-based self-rescues, not one for firefighters who do shore-based agency rescues. Identify the risks where you intend to travel. Understand what specific skill sets you need to manage risk well, and actively seek out training. Remember to pre-plan your trips—plan for the worst and hope for the best.

Practice and Continuing Education

Practice skill sets on a regular basis to maintain proficiency and to avoid complacency. Stay current on new rescue equipment and techniques by getting involved with paddling clubs, books, and resources on the internet.

Judgment and Decision-Making

This simply comes with time and experience. Travel with experienced, talented people to keep your learning curve steep and on track. Debrief all rescue situations to learn from others in your group and to process the complexity of an emergency response. Read up on whitewater accident reports.

Equipment

Good rescues are performed with the right equipment. Know what is reasonable and prudent to carry with you and be sure to have it.

Prevention

Mature rescuers realize that even with all the best equipment and training in the world, tragedies still happen, through no fault of their own. But the best rescue is the one that never happens. Focus on prevention as much as possible and realize it is one of your most important leadership traits.

Stay Calm and Embrace Your Fear
Rescue emergencies can be frightening and emotionally charged. One of the greatest elements a rescuer can bring to the scenario is a cool, calm, and collected demeanor. It can be virtually impossible in some scenarios to eliminate emotional involvement altogether, but spread as much calm as possible in the immediate environment. This doesn't mean you shouldn't be scared. Fear is good.

Fear is a naturally occurring, deeply ingrained, defensive mechanism designed to protect us from danger. The overwhelming sensations we experience are preparing our bodies for battle and our minds for concentration.

There was a popular bumper sticker/T-shirt campaign in the early 1990s using the simple phrase "No Fear." This is but one example of how society has misguided youth's perceptions of fear and adventure sports. Many people will enter the river environment with the impression that fear is an embarrassing trait to have. Instead, embrace your fear.

Paddlers who embrace their fear will admit that they are scared but describe their feelings as extra energy rather than overwhelming nervousness.

Dividing fear into two categories, good fear and bad fear, is another effective tool for shaping our thinking. Bad fear is when confusion, and a lack of specific understanding, allows you to develop anxiety, ill ease, panic, and a frantic demeanor. Good fear is when you recognize fear but do not allow it to overtake your ability to rationalize and perform within your capabilities. Consider avoiding traveling with anyone who says he is not scared of anything or who exhibits a fearless and reckless approach to his whitewater paddling technique.

Always Continue Learning

Perhaps in addition to reading this book, you've also taken a complete swiftwater rescue course but are still feeling a twinge of inadequacy when it comes to certain skill sets. Cherish those feelings, embrace your inadequacies, and use them as fuel to drive you to become more proficient. Realize we never fully arrive at perfection in rescue but spend our lives in relentless pursuit of it. Enjoy this process, and treasure the questions themselves. The real key to success is never being satisfied with your present state of knowledge or ability. Stay hungry for more learning, open to new ideas, and have fun playing in, on, and around rivers.

Index